The Life and Times of "'Por' Little Jimmy"

I0162607

ISBN **978-1-935786-83-2**

Printed in the United States of America

St. Clair Publications
P. O. Box 726
Mc Minnville, TN 37111—0726

http://stclairpublications.com

Cover Design

Kent Grey—Hesselbein Design Studio
www.kghdesignstudio.com

the Life and times of "'por' Little Jimmy"

by

James F. "Jimmy" Stewart

"'Por' Little Jimmy" at age 6 or 7

Dedication

I dedicate this book to all my family members, friends and associates.

I especially want to thank my wife, Mary Louise, for the patience and tolerance during the time I spent researching and writing this book. I also wish to thank her twin sister, Loucille Burdine, for her assistance in this effort.

I want to give special thanks to Katy Overton for transferring this information from my crude handwriting to the computer.

Thanks to family members and friends for any pictures contributed.

I want to thank Fran Johnson for her creation of "'Por' little Jimmy," and Jerry Roper for his portrayal of "'Por' little Jimmy" at a later age.

To all my wonderful friends and especially to all those at Tullahoma First Baptist Church and Sunlake Baptist Church in Lutz, Florida—thank you for your kindness and love. Mary Louise and I feel that we are two of the most blessed people for having so many friends in so many places—

We love every one of you.

James F. (Jimmy) Stewart

November 7, 2013

My Youth

Greetings to everyone who may ever read this. I am setting out to write the true story of my life starting at around 2 years old. My name is James Floyd Stewart, born to John Floyd Stewart and Lelia Bell Sanders Stewart. I was known all my adolescent life as "Por" little Jimmy. When I was somewhere around 2 years old we lived in one hollow, which we called a 'holler' and moved across two hills to another hollow, to the house where we remained until we children were all grown. I'm talking about far back in the back woods of Scott County, Virginia — we moved in an old hand-hewed log house. There were two large rooms with a door on each side of the rooms, and a rock fireplace in each of the rooms. One of these rooms had one window in it; the other room had no windows. So much for those two rooms. Now some time in the past, two more rooms were framed and boxed on both sides and ends with a window and a door in each room leading out on a porch with, of course, an entrance door on one end. Now this porch was extended all the way along the side of the two log rooms. The entrance from one section of the house to the other was by the porch. These two additional rooms were attached to one corner of the log part. We had no electricity and the only running water we had was what came out of the side of the hill and ran down the 'holler.'

Artist's Sketch of Stewart House

You are probably wondering by now why I was known as "'Por' little Jimmy," right? When we moved to the second house, my father was mowing the weeds off the garden and I suppose I was toddling around near where he was mowing the weeds. Anyway, very unfortunately, I fell on a weed he had cut off and it went into my left eye and just completely ruined that eye. We lived so far back in the boondocks, I never was told how they managed this disaster, but somehow they got me to an Ophthalmologist in Bristol, Tennessee/Virginia. The reason I say Bristol, Tennessee/Virginia is that the town had a street through the middle which divided the town; part of it was in Tennessee and part of it was in Virginia. I have to assume my parents must have caught the passenger train of the CC&O Railroad which was some two and half miles from our house and must have ridden it to Mendota, which is about half way between Gate City, Virginia and Bristol. My father had a sister and her family living just outside of Mendota. We spent the night at their house. Uncle Will Vickers, where we spent the night, hooked his horse to his buggy and drove us to Bristol. I don't know how they found the Ophthalmologist because no one had phones back then. We got to the eye doctor and my eye was so mangled there was nothing to do but remove it. We had to go back to the doctor two or three times when the eye socket was healed. The doctor put a small artificial eye in the socket to keep it from closing. Now this little eye, that he happened to have in his stock, was not the correct color but something had to be done to protect the socket for later down the road when my parents could afford the proper artificial eye. I hope you can imagine what this did to my personality and my self-esteem. When we had company I would go to another part of the house and shun being around anyone other than my family. My older brother Ray and my older sister Loraine both were so good to me. Also my father and mother were good to me but, I suppose if I have to be perfectly honest in this story, I would have to say they somewhat spoiled me. The best part of life we had was not wall-to-wall carpet but wall-to-wall love for each other. We really had very little; however I contend we were never poor. The reason I insist that we were not poor is because it takes two o's to spell poor and we could only afford one o. It doesn't take a college mathematician to figure out where that leaves us (p-o-r).

We had 92 acres of hills and 'hollers' and rocks. The way we scratched out a living was with an old gray mare and an old brown mule. It wasn't the most fun thing to plow those hillsides. The gray mare was always about two steps ahead of the lazy mule. When I finally got old enough to go to school, we lived so far back in the hills, that there were only two ways to commute; that was either walk or ride a horse. So we walked about three and half miles to school. We had plenty of snow days back then. They were not like the snow days school kids have today where they get to stay at home. Our snow days back then was walking to school in a foot or two of snow. When I was a kid we would have so much snow we would not see the ground for about two or three months during the winter. When I was about four or five years old I started having rheumatic fever. I would have about 2 seizures from it; one in the spring and one in the fall. I also had rheumatoid arthritis and it would get so bad sometimes that I couldn't walk. One time I recall it got so bad I couldn't even move. My father walked three and a half miles to the little town which was the closest village to us. He got the only doctor there to walk all the way to our house to treat me. I remember very vividly the doctor, after checking me several ways, saying, "Well he's gone." My mother just about went into hysterics. The next day my dad went to the drugstore in the little town to get something the doctor had suggested. As he was walking back home along the CC&O railroad, he ran into an old hobo.

"Can you spare me a bite to eat?" the hobo asked dad. So my kind dad took him on home with him and gave him a good meal. I was still very ill. The hobo then asked my dad about what was wrong with me. Dad told him what my symptoms were.

"One of my kids was like that one time," the old hobo told dad. "The doctor told me to get acid of iron mineral to give my son. I did, and it helped him."

When my dad was back at the drugstore he got me a bottle of acid of iron mineral and they started giving me those vitamins and, sure enough, they helped me!

Many years after that when my adopted son was about 5 or 6 years old he got where he wouldn't eat, and his little legs looked like birds' legs, so I just thought of the acid of iron mineral and got some and put him on them and he started eating and actually got fat.

Now, getting back to "'Por' little Jimmy." I had a miserable time in school; all the other kids could be so cruel and not say a word. I could be walking across the school yard and here would come a bunch of kids; they would put one hand over one eye and kind of bob back and forth and usually would say, "look at ole one eye." I got so put out with talk like that I just started fighting back. I had an old uncle who had just come home from service and I was telling him how cruel and mean to me the other kids were and he took me all the way to the little town of Clinchport, which was near Clinch River. My uncle was dad's brother named James Stewart after whom I was named. On the way to town, Uncle Jim told me and showed me what to do when the other kids started picking on me.

He told me, "Before they even think you might retaliate, just grab them by the hair, one hand on either side of their head and slam their noses down on your knee a couple of times and then slam them down on the ground and kick them and walk off."

We got on into town and there was a walk about 5 or 6 feet high all the way down from the store buildings to the drugstore. We walked to the drugstore and Uncle Jim bought us both a cone of ice cream. We walked back up the walk in front of the big department store and there were three of the boys that had always been mean and cruel to me. One walked right up and knocked my ice cream out of my hand. Of course I cried and the boy got right down in my face saying, "Cry baby, cry baby."

My uncle said right to me, "Now's the time, son, now's the time." I knew what he meant and I grabbed the boy just like Uncle Jim had told me and shown me and slammed his nose down against my knee two or three times and slammed him down on the concrete walk and his head went right down in the ice cream he had knocked out of my hand and messed up his hair. By that time, three or four adults had gathered.

One of the men had said to Uncle Jim, "What did you do to that boy?" and Uncle Jim said, "I didn't do a damn thing to that boy, but my nephew worked him over pretty good for knocking his ice cream out of his hand."

Uncle Jim got me by the hand and said, "Come on son, I think they have some more ice cream down there."

So we went back to the drugstore and he got me another cone of ice cream and we were on our way home, back in the hills. I feel sure that I had more fights and got more whippings in school than probably any two or three of the other boys.

It was that way until I got my first proper artificial eye. Boys would pick on me and I would do what Uncle Jim told me and they would run to the teacher with their noses bleeding and I would get a whipping and they would get sympathy.

Many things had happened before I got that first eye. I lost my father by death much too soon. That left my mother, my older brother Ray, and my older sister Lorraine. Somehow when I was small, in trying to call my sister 'Sissy,' it came out 'Tysie' and my sister went by Tysie virtually all of her life. My mother was 1 of 19 siblings that were his, hers and theirs. There was one half brother and a half sister's husband that were very good to us after my father's death. They would come in the spring and plow the cropland and come in the fall and help harvest the crops.

My mother, bless her dear sweet precious heart, she would go right out into the corn fields, hay fields and tobacco fields and work right along with the men. She would prepare lunch at night and have it just ready to warm up for lunch the next day.

One day Uncle Wright Tipton, my mother's half sister's husband, was at our place to plow some cropland. It rained him out, so he came in from the field and put his horses in the barn. He then came to the house; he and my mother were in the living room talking. I was just outside the front door on the porch playing with the only thing I had to play with. I was not eavesdropping, but it was very easy to hear and understand what they were saying. Oh, I was sitting on the porch setting up Prince Albert Tobacco cans that my dad had smoked the tobacco out of and had saved the cans for me to play with. I would set the cans up in different configurations and push them and watch them fall. I'm sure Uncle Wright was meaning to sympathize with my mother and he kind of attempted to console her. He talked long and drawn out so he said, "Well, Ray is a nice young man; he'll get a good education and a good job and he'll make good in life and Tysie is a beautiful girl, she will probably marry some young man that will make her a good living and they will have a good life, but poor little Jimmy with just one eye, he will never be able to work out in the public. He will have to work out on a farm or back in the back of a restaurant washing dishes or something like that."

I thank the Lord that he made that statement because that motivated me. Right then is when I started leaning on the Lord. I had gone to church quite a bit and I had listened and I understood what prayers were all about so I just said a prayer. I said to myself. "With the help of the Lord, I will show him what 'por little Jimmy' can do." I asked the Lord to lead, guide and direct me and to be my partner in everything that I do. I asked Him to help me to be able to get a good fitting eye, to help overcome my low self-esteem. I even asked Him to show me and tell me just exactly what to do and how to do it. I asked Him to help me to show people what poor little Jimmy can do. I even had the audacity to ask Him to please help me to become a millionaire. I can't say that He has answered all my prayers, but that He sure has answered lots of my prayers. After all that, one day after school, a number of us boys stopped at Bowlings Department Store and I noticed a garbage can was stuffed full and running over on the floor, so I just tramped it all down in the can and picked it up and carried it outside and put it in the big garbage container that would be picked up and hauled off. I went back and just as I set the garbage can back where I had picked it up, Mr. Bowling motioned me to come with him. He said, "How would you like to come by every day after school and do little jobs for me? Do you think your folks would let you do that? If you can, I'll give you a dollar every week."

So I asked my mother about it and she said, "Well, if you want to. What does he want you to do?" she asked.

I said, "All he said was to do little jobs in the store." I did that for three school years and I saved every dollar, then my mother sold a pig or a calf and I went to New York and got my first tailor-made eye. My mother did all this communicating by mail. We went through the original ophthalmologist, Dr. Peevler, and he made the appointment with the eye maker. I went by train and spent the night with the eye maker. He took me the next day and set me right across a little table from him and looked at my good eye and made one just like it. He put me on the passenger train and started me back home. This is really when I started living. People stopped looking at me like I was some kind of a freak and people in general were friendlier and nice to me. I was really proud of my new eye. I sat right in front of the technician with just a small narrow table between us. He was constantly staring at my natural eye and made it just exactly to match my natural eye. Of course the one eye I am using today is an excellent match. Lots of people I come in contact with don't notice the difference in my two eyes.

Music Days

About then was when Carl Tipton and my family and I became good friends. Carl was an excellent musician. Some of you may remember Carl. He had a program for many, many years on the radio station at Murfreesboro, Tennessee. I just suddenly noticed that I'm getting the cart before the horse. I'll go back a few years when we first became good friends. Carl taught me to play the guitar. Carl and I played music together for several years. His sister Ruby would sing with Carl and me. We had not been playing together very long when WKPT in Kingsport had a talent show at the Civic Auditorium. We decided to enter so we went to the radio station and auditioned for the show. We went to the auditorium that night and when our time had come to perform, we went out on the stage; I was scared half to death. When we started performing I started out in the wrong key; however, I caught it right away and got in the proper key and believe it or not, we won second place! After that,

Carl and I played quite a bit until he and his family moved to Murfreesboro; yet Carl and I remained good friends until Carl passed away several years ago. We still remain, until this day, dear friends with Carl's wife, Sophie.

After Carl left Virginia, I just decided to start a Country and Western band. That was the birth of Jimmy Stewart and the Sunset Rangers.

This consisted of Jim Smith, Jay Spangler and Walter and Jack Hanes. Jay Spangler was an outstanding electric Hawaiian guitar player. He also did some very interesting rope tricks. He went by "Tex" Spangler in our little show. We really had a very good show. We played at theaters, high schools and amusement auditoriums.

We had a Saturday afternoon show at WOPI in Bristol. This was way back when Tennessee Ernie Ford was a part time announcer at WOPI. Jay was always complaining about a headache. He died at a very young age.

Jimmy Stewart and the Sunset Rangers. Right to left: Walter Hanes, J. Tex Spangler, Jimmy Stewart, Jim Smith, Jack Hanes.

Jim Smith went on to the Grand Ole Opry and was front man for Carl Smith for several years. Walter Hanes went on to the Grand Ole Opry and substituted for any band that needed help because Walter was a very accomplished musician. He could play any string instrument and play it very, very well. Walter even became producer there for several years.

All of my band has now gone on to the big, big show place. I should say all other than Jack Hanes. I am not sure about Jack. I have not played now for years. I have so much arthritis in my hands now; I can't even make the chords. I have some good friends here that play and we sometimes have a hootenanny at our house.

The Trio of the Band, left to right: J. Tex Spangler, Jimmy Stewart and Jim Smith

I was in Kingsport one Saturday and I saw a big department store that really looked like the one I had worked at for three years in Clinchport. I went into the store and there was just one elderly man there. I looked around a few minutes until I worked up enough nerve to approach the man to ask for a job. I said, "Don't you need a young man with lots of energy to help you here in this big store?"

He said, "Well, in fact, I had thought about it but I don't know of one."

I said, "Well, I have worked in a country department store so I have quite a bit of experience."

He said, "Well what did you do?"

I said, "Well I have swept wood floors and put oil stain on them to help control the dust. I rearranged and dusted and cleaned tables and wall shelves and kept clothes straightened and nice on the tables."

He said, "Well, you sound like you might come in pretty handy here."

I was a big boy, so he didn't even ask me if I had finished school. I was 16 so I thought I would rather work than to go to school, which was kind of silly in a way.

He said, "I can't offer to pay you much. I can only pay you about 20 dollars a week."

Well, to a poor country boy like me, that sounded pretty good. I went to work for him and I really worked well. I even looked for things to do. I had the store, I suppose, the cleanest since it was new. I worked a little more than a year.

Then one day a friend who was in a very good job in town told me that they were looking for a young man at Montgomery Wards. He said, "I've told them about you and they want to talk to you." I went to talk to them and I got the job. I worked for them about 4 years. I was a poor country boy; working in a store didn't seem like work for me, so I looked for something to do. The manager noticed my ability and promoted me to Junior Assistant Manager. I did all the things the manager and assistant manager didn't like to do. Every day's mail brought more and more sheets of directives, such as changing different displays throughout the store. I had to distribute those to the different departments. Also, if someone was out of the department, it was my job to go help in that department. I worked in men's clothes, shoes, hardware and furniture. And if the janitor was out, I even did his job. There was about enough work for about three people, but you guessed it, I actually got the job done. The word got out about me being a good worker and the same week I got a tip that a real estate and insurance company and a 75 year old man in a jewelry store wanted to talk to me. Real estate was always my first choice so I went to the real estate and insurance place. Now I was making 35 dollars a week. The real estate man offered me 50 a week draw against my earnings. I didn't think too much of that offer.

Now about the jewelry store job, I thought, "Well, there really is no use for me to go, but I will at least go and talk to him about it and see what he says." When I went in the store, there were two women in sight, and I introduced myself to the ladies. One said, "Just a minute, I'll get Mr. Lipman."

He came out and said, "Come on with me." We went to the back of the store to his office; then he said, "I hear that you are a good worker."

I told him, "Any job I take I try my best to do as good as, or better than, anyone else before me has done it."

I'll never forget what he said. "I like your attitude. Do you think you would like to work in jewelry?"

My answer was, "Quite frankly, I don't know a thing about jewelry, but I will read and study everything I can find about it."

Again he said, "I like your attitude." He asked me a few more questions and every one I would answer as truthfully as I could and every time, his response was always the same "I like your attitude." He finally told me, "I'm looking for a nice young man that I can teach to take some of the work off me. He paused and looked me in the eye. "I'm old," he continued, "I'm 75 years old."

I spoke up and said, "I will be dependable and I will do my very best."

Again he repeated, "I like your attitude," and then he said the magic word. He said "I think you are what I am looking for. If you want to come and work for me, I will give you 75 dollars a week to start; then if you do well there is more where that came from."

It was good that I was sitting because I think if I had been standing I would have fallen. "I think I would love working for you," I said, "but I feel like I should give two weeks notice."

"I think you should," he told me, "but if for any reason they don't want you to stay two weeks, you come right back here any day and go to work for me."

I didn't say it but I thought "I like your attitude." Well they were happy for me to stay the two weeks and asked me to work full time teaching a young man to do my job. I went to Jordan Jewelers and the old man Lipman was very good to me. I think it was the first of August and everything went very well.

That fall he took me with him to a New York jewelry show to buy merchandise for the Christmas season. In the following spring he took me again to two shows--one in New York and the other in Atlanta. After that he never took me again. He *sent* me! Mr. Lipman only had one daughter and no son. He treated me like he would've treated a son. When I was there about eight months, he came in and said, "Come with me."

I thought, "Uh oh, what have I done wrong?"

We went to his office and sat down. He said, "Are you making it okay on what I'm paying you?"

I said, "Yes, well, I'm living with my sister and her family and they are not charging me very much for rent."

He said, "I'm going to give you a raise of 25 dollars a week on one condition; you are not used to having this extra money, so I want you to start a savings account and save this."

I assured him that I would do just that. In about three months I took my savings book and showed him that I was saving the raise. He gave me another raise. He was very good and kind to me. He gave me a beautiful set of cufflinks that had about a ten point diamond in each one. He said his father gave them to him for his high school graduation. They are now antiques. I still have them and I treasure them very highly. I haven't worn them for a few years because French cuffs have been out for several years now. I think I will see if I can find French cuff shirts so I can wear them again. At that time he had only been coming in the store after he had lunch with his brother Henry Lipman who had the Jewel Box store across the street. My Mr. Lipman's first name was Adolf.

"'Por' Little Jimmy" Goes in Business

Several years went by and I had taken a vacation and gone to see my brother and mother in Louisville, Kentucky. On Sunday, my brother Ray drove me around to see the town since I had never been there before. I saw a help wanted ad on a jewelry store window, so I went back downtown on Monday. Their ad wanted an assistant manager for their store in Paducah, Kentucky. I went back to Kingsport and turned in my notice. I stayed there an additional month and went to Paducah. I had kind of been wanting to go somewhere else for a while anyway. I was at Paducah a little over a year. There were two brothers from Chattanooga that I had met in a New York Jewelry market; they had a jewelry wholesale in Chattanooga and several jewelry stores around there in Georgia, Alabama and Tennessee. They found out somehow to contact me. They wanted me to go thirds with them on a store in Tullahoma, Tennessee. A man from Mississippi had come there when a large government project, AEDC, came to Tullahoma. He had put a nice beautiful jewelry store there. He had gone broke and we bought his stuff for ten cents on the dollar and took over his lease. We agreed to let him stay there through December. We bought it in November of 1951. I bought with the understanding and had it in the contract that if I ever wanted out of the business we would inventory it and they would pay me fair market value for my third. This will sound like I am bragging but I have earned the right to brag about it. I was there twelve plus years and I increased the business each year over the year before.

While I was in Tullahoma, a group of us business men did minstrel shows for the Lion's Club. Professor Stamps of the Black school there was actually our biggest supporter.

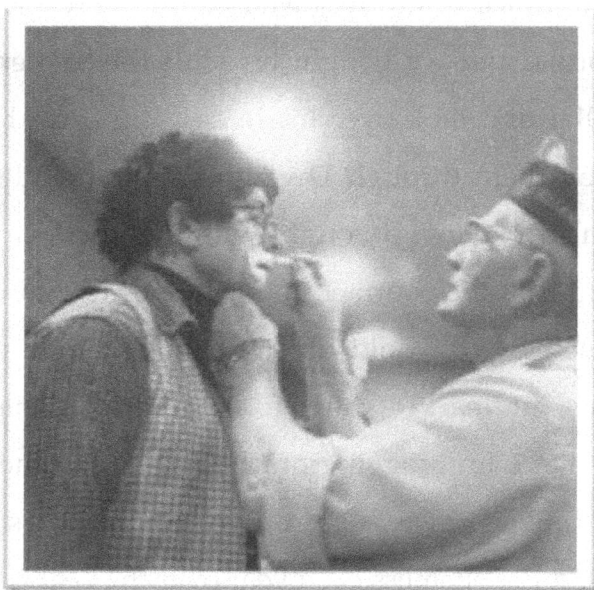

Jimmy Having Makeup Applied for a Minstrel Show

Jimmy in Minstrel Show

Now with the sudden change in my life, I met a nice beautiful young lady named Dean Ferrell. When we married in 1963, I sold my share of the business and we went to Kingsport, Tennessee. I had a good friend there who I palled around with when we were young. We had always discussed getting into some business together and we had the opportunity to take on a dealership for John Deere--both industrial and agricultural equipment. The owner/partnership was that he would manage the office and shop and financing and I was to build up a sales force and handle sales. This started in 1963. We were doing very well. Things were going great. I had employed eight salesmen.

I had been working with a logging group in Roan Mountain. On a Monday morning I thought I had not seen the Roan group for a couple of weeks, so I figured I should go there to keep contact. When I got there I discovered that just at closing time on Friday, they had a log skidder and a twenty ten loader to quit on them. I ended up that morning selling them three machines and taking their two duds in trade. I had executed a very profitable transaction and I went back in the office with the intent of having the unit serviced that I had sold and for my partner to get the financial papers all taken care of so we could get the equipment to the loggers because they were really in need of them.

When I got to the office, just as I entered the front door, the parts department was immediately on my left. I asked the parts man if Bob Addington was in. The parts man said, "Yes, he is in his office," so I turned right and went down the hall to his door. It was locked. I knocked, but no response. I knocked and I knocked. Finally I went back and said, "Bob isn't in his office. Do you know where he went and when he'll be back?"

The parts man said, "He is in there. Is he sick or something?" Then he said, "If he isn't now, he probably will be."

I went back and knocked and knocked furiously, there was no response. I went to the shop and got a wrecking bar and jabbed and pried the door open.

When the door opened I knew what was wrong. The smell of whiskey would've knocked you down. I shook and shook him and could not wake him up. I proceeded to give the shop foreman the numbers of the three units I had sold. I told them to tell Bob if he wakes up before closing time to meet me at 8:00 in the morning. If he doesn't wake up to call his wife and tell her to tell him to meet me at the office. About a quarter past 8:00 o'clock he came in looking about half asleep. Bags under his eyes, he said, "Well the finance man and the John Deere field man were here and I think they put something in my drink." Then he turned right around and told what had happened. He said "If you don't want to wine them and dine them, you won't get merchandise."

Then I told him, "If that is what it takes, I am in the wrong business." Bob and I had gone lots of places together. Even gone out with crowds to dances and practically all the others were drinking. Neither Bob nor I would take a drink and would not chip into their buying drinks. Anyway, time went on and after that, things just didn't mesh. I was told later that Bob was still selling Ford cars and trucks and not sharing the proceeds. I just finally told Bob that I thought we should resolve our partnership.

He said, "Well, we were doing good; I don't see why we should mess the business up." I approached him two or three times asking to decide a price that he would give me for my half or the price he would take for his half. Finally, I just told him that we were dissolving our partnership. "How do you want to do it? We can do it personally or let the court settle it?" I really believe that he thought I wanted to buy it but I didn't. He finally came up with an offer to buy or sell, and it was a fair offer, so I sold to him and we went back to Tullahoma.

I then went into the real estate business with Earl Shahan. There were about nine or ten salespeople, so we kind of took turns staying a day in the office.

One morning early I happened to be in the office and my sister called me. She never called me early like that, so I knew something was wrong. I asked her what it was.

She said, "Are you sitting down?" She didn't wait for a response before she said, "Bob Addington committed suicide last night!"

Not too long after that I just happened to be in the office again and the younger Shulman brother from the jewelry business in Chattanooga said, "Al and I are coming to Tullahoma. After all, we haven't seen you in a long time and we would like to buy you lunch."

"Call me when you are ready," I said. They called about 11:30 and we met at Vi's Restaurant. Vi was a nice old African-American lady and the food was always good there. We talked about a little of everything. The older brother Al asked me, "How would you like to be back in the jewelry business?"

I said, "Well I've been out long enough till I don't feel like a bird in a cage anymore." They ended up offering to give me a third interest in the business if I would take it back over. I was doing quite well in real estate so I turned it down. They had tried three or four people since I left and the jewelry business had gone way down. I really think I could've built it back up again, but I was happy in real estate.

From Tragedy to Triumph

It was now up to 1967. On December 17th, my wife was killed in an automobile accident leaving me with an adopted son that just turned eight years old. In order to try and keep him happy I bought a skating rink. He loved to skate so well, but he met a real cute little girl there who came from a not too stable or sound family.

Her mother readily consented to her little girl going and living with Tim and me. She sure was a blessing to both of us. She was a good child and was a great help to me with the house cleaning and even the cooking. We are, until this day, still visiting friends with Dean's brother and his wife and his family.

After about three years, Tim's grandmother wanted him to come and live with them. But you know the influence grandparents can have on young children. Tim went to live with them and Billie went back home. That left me there with an empty house and it got so lonely and so sad there all alone that I just prayed and asked the Lord to please send me a companion. I even gave specifications like a good Christian country girl that was raised like I was and, thank the Lord, He answered my prayer verbatim. He gave me my beautiful sweet wife Mary Louise Hefley, now Stewart. She is so sweet and good to me I don't know how in the world I could ever do without her. We still have a very close relationship with Billie and her nice husband and their cute little girl. Mary Louise and I both love them greatly. We also love Tim very much; however, we have not seen or heard from him for a long time. I would like very much to have a good father-son relationship with Tim. All I can do now is pray.

The Lord has been so good to us; I have worked and prayed and prayed and worked to try to save for retirement. Even while I was in jewelry I did real estate trading. I had bought several houses and farms when I finally got into real estate which was my first love from the time I was very young. After Mary Louise and I got married, I decided to slow down a little. I thank the Lord for His many blessings and so many answered prayers. He hasn't answered all my prayers, but He has answered a lot of very important ones. I frequently think that Mary Louise and I are two of the most fortunate people in the world. We have 38 plus years of the most wonderful, beautiful, harmonious life together. We don't owe anything, other than taxes, insurance, lights and water. We are fortunate enough to have a home in Tullahoma,

Tennessee where we live in the summer and a home in Lutz, Florida where we spend, hopefully, all of the cold weather. We love it when we are here and we love it when we are there. We have a host of friends in Lutz and Tampa and we have a host of friends in Tullahoma. We are so fortunate that both Mary Louise and I have such wonderful families. We both dearly love each other's family. We are now trying to decide where to settle down for living full time. We have our house here in Lutz. Our lot goes back to a wonderful fishing lake and goes over a small portion about 50 feet and takes in the end of a small island. I built a bridge across to the island and a covered picnic pavilion with an enclosed kitchen, refrigerator and gas cook stove. We enjoy it very much. We have our church friends over for picnics. It seats 50 people. Fishing is great. I have caught catfish and bass as long as my arm.

I will make several pages with nothing but pictures but I am going to change the scene now. I am going to tell you a funny that a buddy and I did. Way back when I was at Montgomery Wards I took a mannequin home with me. We dressed it up and tied a long rope to it, put the rope over a tree limb and pulled it to bring the mannequin up and down. Then there was a revival at a church way out in the country. There were several people that traveled this particular country road. We picked out a place in the road that kind of curved around a little high hill that showed up real good. So we set our mannequin beside a tree at the top of the hill where it showed up in plain sight to the people walking the curve. We left church early and when the people started coming around the curve, we would pull the rope and move the mannequin up, then let it down for a few times and we would just leave it low until everyone had left. Then we just took it down and left. There was a lot of talk about it for several days.

Modern Woes and Wows

Now I will get back to "Por' little Jimmy." About four years ago I had to have my left knee replaced and then before it got completely well I fell and broke my left hip. Now I am walking with a walker and I am having a dizziness problem. My doctor prescribed medication, and I took the whole prescription two different times, but with no results. I am still dizzy. Now I'm also having trouble with my right knee. I went to an orthopedic doctor and he said they had found a new kind of medication to give by a shot in the knee. They didn't have it on hand, so they ordered it. They said it would be about four to six weeks coming in. I'm anxious to get the shot because the doctor said they were having very good success from the shots. Right now I am just sitting in my lift recliner with both legs lifted up; however, I do quite a bit of exercise when Mary Louise goes to the grocery or drug store. While she shops I walk the floors; they are perfect for walking with my walker. I walk on the inside, around the inside wall. That is the best place I have found to walk.

Well, I have to stop writing for a while, Mary Louise just let in a big black and white kitty cat; he is a beautiful sweet cat; he's a community cat. I guess he was originally dropped off three or four years ago; now he just goes around the neighborhood; everyone loves him and feeds him. He only comes in when Mary Louise will bring him in. He will come straight to me and jump up in my lap. He likes for me to pet him. Since he's black and white, someone tagged him with the name of Tuxedo.

We love pets but the way we travel around, we can't have them. When we are here we look forward to going back to Tullahoma. When we are in Tullahoma, we look forward to coming back here to Lutz. When we are in Tennessee in the summer we go to Arkansas to visit Mary Louise's family and my family in east Tennessee and Virginia, what is left of them. I have a first cousin, Claymon Stewart, and his wife Serena.

When Claymon and I both became the only ones of our immediate families, we declared ourselves brothers. We have been about as close as brothers. Mary Louise and I love both of them like brothers and sisters. I also have a niece and her husband, Patty and Joe Blevins that live in Palm Harbor, Florida, about 30 minutes away. We see them quite often; they have one son Max and a daughter Tracy and her husband, Mark. They have good spouses; each one has one spizwart and one mugwomp. Just for your information, all little girls are spizwarts and all little boys are mugwomps. Mary Louise and I love them dearly. I think without a doubt when we get old enough that we will not need or want to alternate, that we will be staying here in Lutz permanently. Then we will see our family members more. We have some commercial property in Tullahoma that we will need to dispose of before moving full time. We may or may not sell our house there. We have one other residential house left, and I'm not sure what we'll do about it.

About four years ago, a young man was working for me keeping up properties. He was an excellent worker. He did carpenter work, electrical and plumbing. He was buying a rental, a three bedroom house on two acres just outside of Tullahoma. All of a sudden he began to complain about headaches. When he went to the doctor a huge mass was found on his brain. They decided it was too large to try to take all out at one time so thus far he has had three brain surgeries. Now all that is left is a fourth of the part of the mass that is embedded down in the brain. They have given all the different cancer treatments hoping they may find something that might help. One good thing is that it's not cancer. They have not told the patient or anyone that I know of they are not doing surgery on it. I think I have figured it out. They think the surgeons know if they try to remove it from the brain that he will die on the operating table, or if he lives he will be a vegetable. He just had his 35th birthday a few months ago. He has not been able to do anything for about three or four years. He and his wife have three children. The wife is not a well person. She had, I think, two surgeries last year and the first of this year. We feel so sorry for them. We are just letting them live there free. I don't know if we can claim any of that on our income tax or not.

However, that's not the important part. I feel the Lord has been so good to us I think He expects us to do something for someone who is no longer able to do anything for himself. I thank the good Lord several times every day for being so good to Mary Louise and me. I thank Him every day for every year of my life, for every month, day, week, hour and minute, second and for every breath of life that He has blessed Mary Louise and me with. Mary Louise is quite a bit younger than I am. When people ask me my age, I tell them to hang whatever numbers might fit; be it too many or too few. I'll wear them just as graciously as I can.

We have a wonderful small church just across the north/south highway from where we live. It's just two houses off the east/west road that runs into the north/south highway; probably about ten0 minutes from our house. Mostly older people belong; however they are a wonderful Christian group of people. We love going there. We love the wonderful minister and his wife. We have some really great friends there. We also have a marvelous church in Tullahoma. It is a fairly large church with a wonderful pastor plus three associate pastors, a minister of music, a great quartet and two male quartets. We also have a ladies trio. They are all very good. We also have an orchestra. We have two Sunday services. One at 8:00 AM and one at 11:00 AM. There is a lot of talent in the church. We also have many good personal friends. Mary Louise and I love them all; male, female, big, little, young and old.

I started a wonderful little deal with all of the women and teenage girls; I tell them I need a lot of heart therapy. Heart therapy equates to a hug. It is a joy and a lot of fun. I contend that is the way I can show my Christian love. It works well; it's a good ice breaker and a good way to make friends. I haven't told you, but Mary Louise and I met in a single adult Sunday school class while playing a game of Aggravation. I have been aggravating her for over 38 years now. Thank the good Lord.

Jimmy & Mary Louise STEWART

Tullahoma TN ● 931 455-9031
Lutz FL ● 813 949-6339

WELCOME TO
First Baptist Church of Tullahoma
108 East Grundy Street, Tullahoma TN 37388 • 931 455-5461
Sunlake Baptist Church
18908 Sunlake Blvd., Lutz FL • 813 949-9248

I am putting one of our personal cards here in the face side. You will see Mary Louise and my pictures from our church album and Tullahoma with our address and phone numbers of both churches and both of our homes. On the backside there is a prayer I wrote when I was 21 or 22 years old called "Toiler's Prayer." The prayer goes like this:

Lord, as I face this working day
help me in all I do or say,
to be a Christian true four square
and treat my fellow men
and fellow workers fair and square.
Let me turn in a full day's work,
and from no job or duty shirk.
When this day comes to an end,
please bring me safely home again.

It has been my working creed all my working life. If I go out to do anything pertaining to our property, for years I would just tell people the prayer, but quite a few years ago I started putting it on the back of my cards. I like to give my cards to people and suggest they memorize it. I especially enjoy giving them to young people just starting their life and business. I don't claim there is anything magic about it, but it sure will keep you thinking if you use it. I am very proud of it. My wife and I always have a complete physical every year. I've been kidding my doctor for several years. I say, "I am gonna live to be 100 in spite of all you doctors." Last fall when I went back for the consultation on my physical, he looked at all the paperwork and said, "Well everything's exactly where it's supposed to be, so keep doing what you're doing and wear your seatbelt and I think you'll make it." Thank God! He has taken very good care of me.

I must not end this without telling about a man that works for us in our real estate. He has been working for us some eight or nine years now. His name is Gino Floreni. He takes care of our rental properties. I really appreciate him and I feel very comfortable coming to Florida and leaving everything in his care. I don't think he would be any more concerned about the care of the rental real estate if he actually owned it himself. I'm thinking seriously of making him a gift of a commercial lot there in Tullahoma. It really already has water and sewer taps and is worth $12,500. We will be in Lutz on just the north end of Tampa until the end of March. I am hoping the economy will have picked up a little by then, for I plan to have an auction sale for our commercial property. It is about time I should be completely retired instead of semi-retired.

The Lord sent me to Tampa, Florida in 1974 to spend the winter. That's how the Lord brought us together. In the singles class, we met in the winter of 1974. We married the 26th of August, just two days after my birthday on the 24th. It didn't take her long to talk me into marrying her. I think we both knew that God had put us together. I knew right away that she was an answer to my prayer because I found out right away that she was what I had asked God for. She was raised up kind of like I was but not as "por". She was a country product like I was. She was a Christian like I asked for and she even loves music like I asked Him. I doubt there is a couple in the country that has gotten along as well as we have. We had an understanding before we married. We agree that everyone is entitled to their opinion even if it is wrong. I have different opinions at different times; however, we didn't ever let them go into a quarrel or even a heated argument.

We worked in the singles class for quite a while after we married when we were here in Florida in the winters. When we went back to Tullahoma, after we married, I was president of my Sunday school before I went to Tampa in 1974. When we came back to Tullahoma I told Mary Louise that we would go to all the churches and we would join the one where she felt most comfortable. She was an employee in the First Baptist Church in Tampa when we met. We started out visiting the First Methodist, then two or three others, when we went to First Baptist. When we started up the steps, three greeters came running down the steps to greet us. They just took us over to our Sunday school classes. We joined the church and very soon it was announced in the morning service that Reverend Hubert Wooten, who was conducting services on Sunday mornings at the life care nursing home, needed a piano player and someone to help patients come from their rooms to the church services which were held in the dining room. We worked there for about three or four years during the summer while we were in Tullahoma.

Then we decided that our church should have a singles class. We went to the pastor and presented the idea to him. He readily agreed and told us to proceed. The first Sunday we met as a singles class we had secured a wonderful Christian lady to teach. That Sunday it was Mary VanZant, Mary Louise and me. Each Sunday after, we gained students until we had twenty some and when we would have a singles affair of some kind we would have thirty to forty attend. We were with that church several years after Mrs. VanZant felt that she could no longer teach. We got a very fine teacher, Jerry Spurlin, who taught the class lessons for several years and we just more or less moved out of the singles, however, I think the singles still exist there. Mary Louise is still on call for the piano playing if they have no one else. Until I broke my hip, I was more or less a freelance greeter. In other words we are still very regular in the church when we are in town. We both love people.

We started something several years ago. You know how it is after a couple has been married some time there is nothing either spouse needs. We decided to use the birthday, anniversary and Christmas money for each other to buy something for some needy person or family. We have now been doing this for several years. This is something we can do together and we enjoy this more than racking our brains trying to think of something for each other. You should try that sometime, it is very gratifying.

Some Memories of the Past

I'm going to tell you another funny; however this time this funny is one on me. I told you earlier about buying the skating rink for the kids after my first wife died. I had a family that operated the business for me; however, I would go by it quite frequently. I became friendly with a very attractive girl that spent quite a bit of time in the evenings in the skating rink. She was also a waitress one block away. We became very friendly and started going places together. One Saturday we were planning to go dancing that night so she said she would go home when she got off from work and asked me to pick her up. She gave me the directions to pick her up. When I knocked on her door, a lady came out; I spoke to her and said, "I'm here to pick Kathy up."

When Kathy came out and we got in the car, she laughed and said, "You know what mom said when she told me you were here? She said 'you're not going out with that old man are you? I dated him before you were ever thought of!' I told her that you were nicer to me than the young boys I've been dating."

If I remember correctly I believed this happened in 1974 before I went to Tampa. She was a very attractive and sweet girl, however, after I met Mary Louise, I knew immediately she was the answer to my prayer. Mary Louise is not only a dear Christian and a good wife; she is literally a living, walking answered prayer. We are in Florida now and we're having beautiful pleasant weather.

I was in a very serious auto accident in the 1960s that came close to taking me away from here. A young boy ran into me on my side of the road. It busted my head right thru both ears. I had two skull fractures, broken collarbone and shoulder blade, ruptured three discs in my back, broke both legs between the knees and foot and dislocated my left hip. I still have a steel plate in my head. I cannot stand cold weather. I'm like the bunny rabbit. I'm kicking and keep on ticking. I was unconscious 28 days and in the hospital 48 days. I was several months recuperating. I feel sure that it was strictly the will of my partner, the Lord Jesus Christ, that I am here today.

I have had the audacity again to ask God to answer another prayer. I have been praying for God to please let me live to be 100 years old and I have the faith to believe that He will do that. If He grants me this prayer, after that I will only ask that His will be done. If this happens I plan to have a huge party and let this be your personal invitation.

I'm going to tell you another funny. Oh boy. There's a possible chance that a couple of words could be thought of as slang, however, please don't read a different word instead of the word I use. This, I suppose, was when I was around 13 years old. I had a buddy also the same age. There was a revival at the same church way back in the country where I told the story about the mannequin. Going to the church, there were about three or four gates to go through.

As you go to church the sliding gate latches were on the side of the gate right in front of you. It was quite easy to just take hold of the sliding latch and slide it back and open the gate, however, as you were coming from the church it was different situation as you had to put your hand through the higher slats in the gate, reach down some eight to ten inches and take hold of the sliding latch to open it. There were two or three very pretty girls 15 to 17 years old that travelled that route every night after revival. My friend and I loved to walk along in the company of these girls. We would be nice and open the gates and hold them open for the girls. We would have courted them if we had known how. After the first two or three nights, young guys began walking these girls home. My buddy and I thought of a meanie we planned to do the last night of the revival. Of course other people, the older people, went on ahead and there were perhaps ten minutes between the old folks and the courting couples. My buddy and I got just behind the old folks and we proceeded to pick up a stick and get the cow droppings on our sticks and smear all over every one of the gate latches. There was only one way to get to the latches. That was to put your hand and arm through the higher slats of the gates and we had doctored them. We went like the good little boys that we were. We went up and walked along with the old group.

There was quite a bit of discussion about it for several weeks after that. We were very sorry that we couldn't hide near any of the gates to observe the reaction. Ha ha. There were a few little antics we did later on; however, we were still pretty good boys. We didn't do anything that really hurt people or cost them any real expense. A few times during trick or treat we turned over a few neighbors' outhouses. We didn't, or at least I didn't, have any fear of them sneaking over and turning our outhouse over because we were so "por" we didn't even have one of them.

The Little Farm

In addition to our home here in Lutz, we have a small six and one half acre farm about 45 minutes north of us in Pasco County. I looked for two years for a small tract of land. I would watch the ads in the newspaper here called *The Flyer*. Anytime I saw something that I thought I might be able to afford, when I would go look at it; if it wasn't already half covered with water, it was obvious that when it rained that it would be covered with water. Finally I found this small acreage in the shopper and I went to see it. A young man had inherited it, and nothing had been done on it for 14 years. To say the least, it was a mess. It had bushes, briars, and all kinds of undesirable growth. It fronted a dirt country road and had just a very small elevation above about half way up the slope then had about the same degree down the other half of the back. The only water on that was a well. I really don't think you could tell the difference in the taste of that well water and bottled water. The country road has now been black topped and just about a couple hundred feet across the side street there is a real nice subdivision and a nice 18-hole golf course. Now there was an old dilapidated house there that had a septic tank tested sufficient for a three bedroom, two bath home. I got a man with a bulldozer to clean the whole six and one half acres. I proceeded to build a four-foot woven wire fence around it. Then I bought a 14-foot wide mobile home with one and one half baths and put it where the dozer had taken the old house down. We rented it for 2 or 3 years. Of course when one would move out, Mary Louise and I would have to go up and clean it up. The last time we went up to clean it, when we pulled up in the drive and got out, fleas covered our legs. We went to the drugstore and a department store and got bombs to put off inside and insecticide granules to spread all outside.

Well, we got rid of the fleas, but Mary Louise said, "Now I don't want to continue with this; I want you to sell it." Well, to appease her, I put a very small for sale sign on a tree about 200 feet up the hill where I thought it would not even be seen. And lo and behold, about a month later a mortgage broker saw it and called me. I really had not even thought about a price to ask for it.

He said, "I like your place and would like to buy it if you would be willing to owner finance it with a down payment. I can easily pay the monthly payments on it."

I had to do some pretty fast thinking. I really didn't want to sell it, so I thought I would put it so high that he wouldn't want it. He still had not asked me the price of it. I had been in real estate long enough to know how to handle things like that. I just told him hold the phone and I would be right back. I just got my rate book and looked for a price that the payments would sound interesting so I settled for $85,000. He would pay $10,000 down; his payments were to be $650 for 20 years. I still had not told him the price of the property. I just come back and on the phone and said, "Well, the monthly payments are very easy; they are only $650 per month." He said, "Oh yeah, that will be no problem." It was not until he came down to my house to close the deal that I told him the price. We put it on a contract until he had paid more on it. He paid about 3 years and he came by and asked me if he'd paid $25,000 more if I would give him the deed. I put it on 15 years instead of 20 years so his payments and taxes and insurance were still around $550. We had set it up for him to deposit the payments in our bank down here. He paid another 5 years and one month.

Mary Louise said, "Pete didn't deposit his payment the first of this month, you ought to call him."

I said, "No, just leave it alone, if he doesn't pay the first of the next month, we'll foreclose on him."

Just in a few days a state's attorney called me and said, "We believe we have information on a fraud concerning a mortgage you hold on a piece of property you have in Pasco County."

The mortgage broker we sold it to was locked up in prison. He sold that piece of property to six different people; one of them being his wife's parents. Of course I had to get a real estate attorney and the property went thru court. It cost me only what the lawyer charged and back taxes that had not been paid.

The first one he had sold it to was living in it. He had remodeled the mobile home and built around it and made it into a house. He had built an addition onto a barn there and made a cabinet shop. He is a professional cabinet maker. He has been our renter ever since we repossessed it. He is behind on his rent from back sometime. He wants to buy the farm from me but I told him I wouldn't even discuss the sale of it to him until he catches up the back rent. I still don't want to sell it. Perhaps sometime down the road.

Let's Go Back a Bit

I should've told you why I came to Florida in the first place. I think it was around the middle part of 1972. A man and his wife came into my real estate office one morning wanting to buy some land. I showed them all we had listed. None was what they wanted.

I said, "You have been describing a parcel of land that I own but it really isn't on the market. We will pass it as we go back to the office." But when we got to it, it was so close to the city limits you could see the marker on it and then it went back to a creek. That was what they had been describing all the time.

The wife spoke up and said, "This is what we are looking for," so I wound up trading them 13 acres and a very small house for one huge house just across the street from the Hillsborough River and a smaller house downtown plus a commercial lot in Rosemont, California, plus a Mercedes Benz automobile.

In 1974 a pickup truck ran into me and bashed me up quite a bit, so I went to Tampa to recuperate a little. I haven't told you about that before, however, I lived in the smaller house in 1974; then when we got married we lived in it one winter.

Then I bought a very nice 3 bedroom, 2 bath house in the north part of town. We lived in it till 1981 when I built the house we are living in now. During that winter one of the first dear friends I met in 1974 at First Baptist Church was a professional architect. I drew the rough sketch of our house and he put it to scale. Both he and his dear wife are in heaven now, I'm sure. We built the house in the winter of 1981. I had several carpenters, plumbers and electricians. I supervised the whole operation. I stayed very close to be sure the insulation was sufficient. After the exterior walls were up and the windows and doors were in, I took the insulation and chinked it all around the doors and windows and around the switches and plugs. Then after the insulation was in the walls, I had aluminum insulation tacked over the whole wall. Then before the sheet rock was tacked to the ceiling, I personally put the Denny foil on the upside of the ceiling sheet rock. Also, I put the aluminum sheets on the concrete floor before the floor covering was put down. I have reason to believe that our house is probably the best insulated house in the whole area. We have checked with several other homeowners with houses about the same size as ours. We find that our utility bill runs around one quarter to one third less than the average. The way I see it was that the insulation has really paid off well. Our house is very easy to heat and cool.

Our Present Blessings

It is now Thanksgiving morning. At our prayer time we discussed all the things that we had to be thankful for. I really think if I concentrated on it enough that we probably could fill a couple of pages of our book just with these blessings. We are going over to our niece and nephew's house in Palm Harbor in just a few minutes. We are spending Thanksgiving with them. Patty and Joe are such wonderful good people and they are so good to Mary Louise and me. They both keep busy. Patty volunteers at the hospice thrift store and Joe is an officer in the Coast Guard and he has some rental property. He always seems busy as a cat on a tin roof. However, he never gets too busy; if we need them they always come to our rescue.

Okay, we are at Patty and Joe's for Thanksgiving dinner. Patty is an excellent cook and she always cooks enough for two or three times as many as will be there. Their son and his sweet wife and also their spitzwart and mugwomp are here. They are such good children. They are a family that is very easy to love. Now it will take me, with Mary Louise helping, a couple of weeks to lose the extra pounds I put on there. I used to struggle to keep my weight down to 200 after I broke my hip; however, I have lost a lot of weight. I figured with my hip and a bad knee that I needed to keep my weight down around 175 pounds and by no means let it get over 180. I have been running around 175 to 179 pounds. I weigh early in the morning with only my pajamas on. I will have to cut my portions down now.

Patty and Joe's children and grandchildren will be going to Kingsport, Tennessee for Christmas. They still own Patty's home place there. I think they are having pretty strong thoughts of selling it. I wish them luck.

I will tell you now how the shot the doctor gave me in my knee has worked out. I went back to him just this early afternoon. Today I was very sorry to report to him that the shot did not do one thing for my knee. It is now 7:00 PM and my knee is really uncomfortable. Especially when I am standing up on it or when I am walking on it. He told me that there is a special healing ointment that is said to be very good and he will also order it like they did the shot. Well, to say the least, I sure hope it does better than the shot did because the shot did nothing.

Well, I didn't do any writing during the holidays. It is now January 14th. A very nice lady from the church where we go had come over one day before Christmas and did a section of my writing on her word processor. She is the pastor and his wife's daughter. She will be back over in a few days and process some more. Well, Christmas and New Year's holidays are both over and gone and I am kind of glad, for the only meaning Christmas has for me anymore is the real true meaning that we all should celebrate everyday of our lives whether they are many or few; and that is the birth of our Savior Jesus. After all, we are in His hands. I am a firm believer if you are faithful to Him and serve Him as we should that He will be good and generous with us. I wish everyone who ever reads this story of my life, a God blessed, healthy and happy prosperous remainder of a very long life. I want to solicit each of your friendships. No one can ever have too many friends. I want now to pray for each one of you. *Lord Jesus I thank you for every blessing of life. I thank you for blessing all of us so abundantly, financially, physically, spiritually, mentally and materially. Talk to their hearts Lord; guide them in your pathway. If it is within your will, please bless them all as you have blessed me. Amen.*

Your friend, James F. "Jimmy" Stewart.

P.S. My last words of advice for us all, just remember today is the first day of the rest of our lives. Let us all serve the Lord and He will make the best of it for all of us.

FAMILY ALBUM

**Jimmy's Great-grandparents, Robert Shaw Stewart
and Nancy Andrews Stewart**

Jimmy's Paternal Grandfather, James Robert Stewart

Jimmy's Maternal Grandparents,
William Wesley "Billy" Sanders and Eliza J. Tyler Sanders

Jimmy's Father, John F. Stewart

Jimmy's Mother, Lelia Sanders Stewart Calhoun
and Stepfather, William L. Calhoun

Jimmy; his Mother; Brother, Ray and Sister, Tysie

Jane, Janet, Ray and Betty

(Phil, out of sight. peeping out of the bush)

Jimmy's Mother, Called "Mamaw"

Ray's Children: Phil, Betty and Janet

Jane, Phil, Ray, Tysie, Jimmy and Ray's Mother

Jimmy's Brother, Ray in Military Uniform

Ray's Wife, Jane Lane Stewart in Younger Days

Jimmy and Wife, Mary Louise, 2009

Jimmy's First Wife, Dean Ferrell Stewart

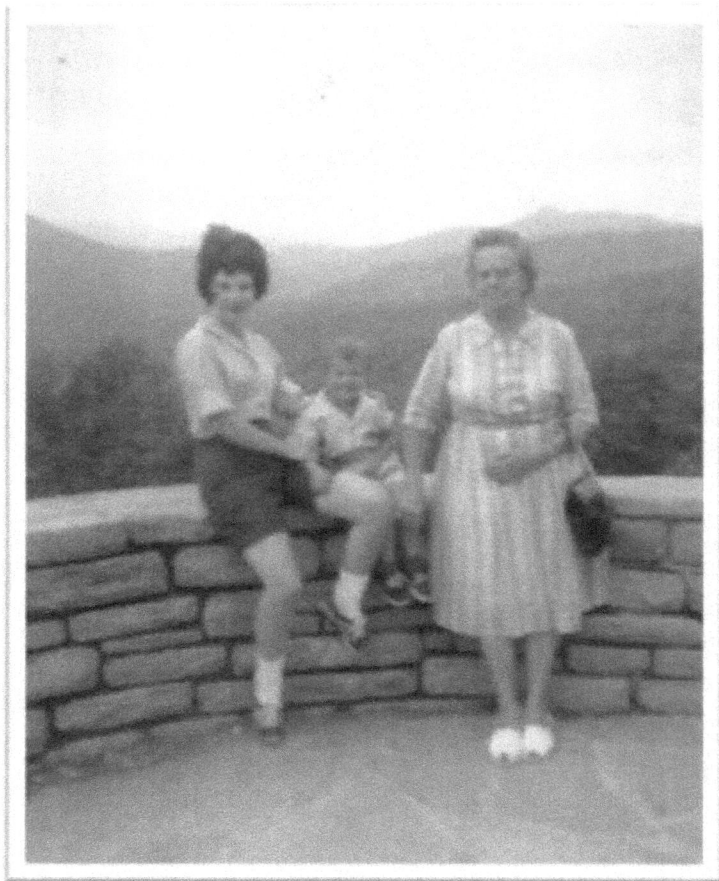

Dean, Tim and Lela, Jimmy's Mother

Tim as a Young Child

Two More Pictures of Young Tim

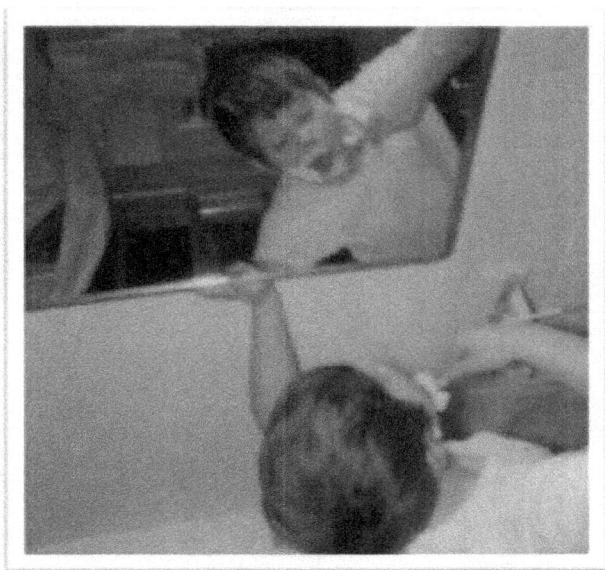

Tim Acting Like He Was Shaving

School picture of Tim

Dean's Brother, Dorris Ferrell and His Wife, Stanka

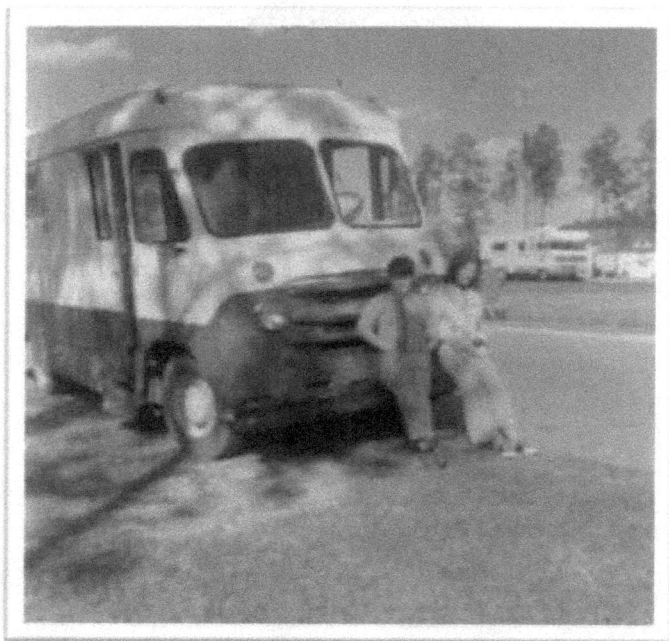

Tim and Billie with Camper Going to Florida

Jimmy and Mary Louise, 1975

Mary Louise and Rowdy, 1992

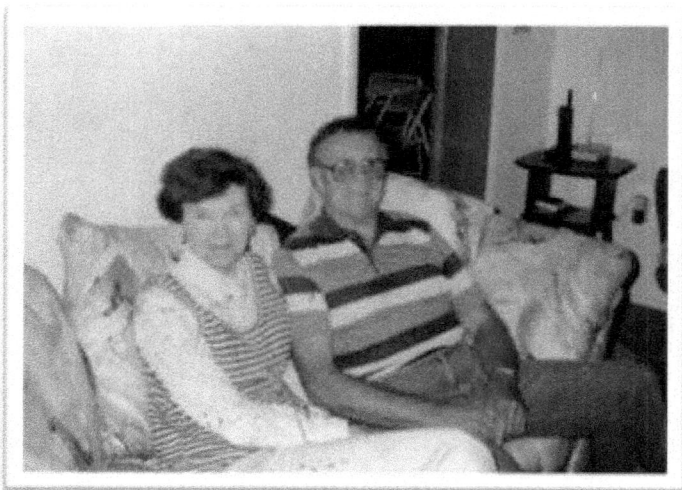

Jimmy and Mary Louise, Lutz, Florida, 1998

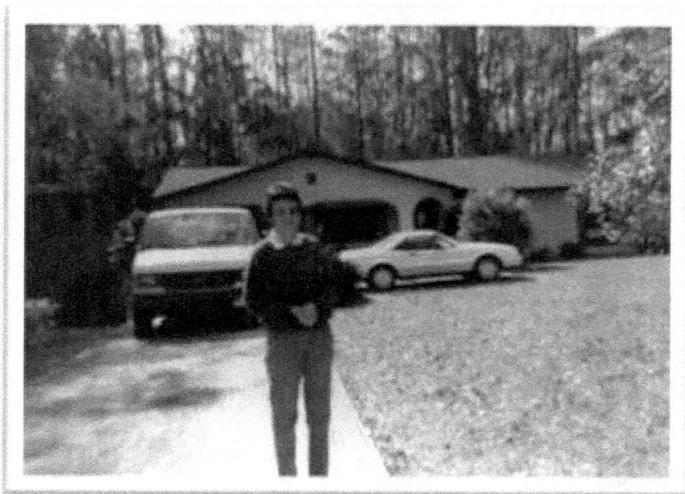

Mary Louise in Front of Florida Home, 2009

Jimmy's Mother, Lela

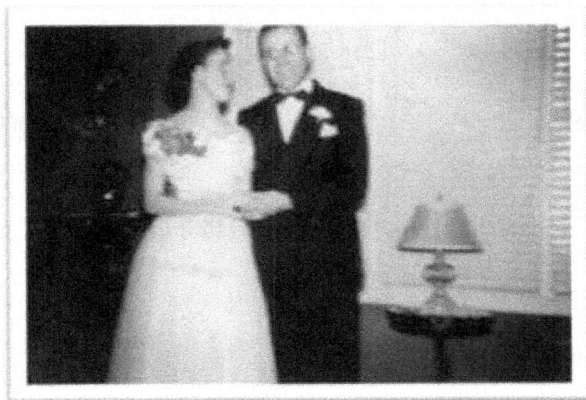

Jimmy and Niece, Shirley Lawson Shepard, at Her Wedding

Jimmy's Sister, Lorene (Tysie) and Husband, Duard Lawson

Front of House in Tullahoma

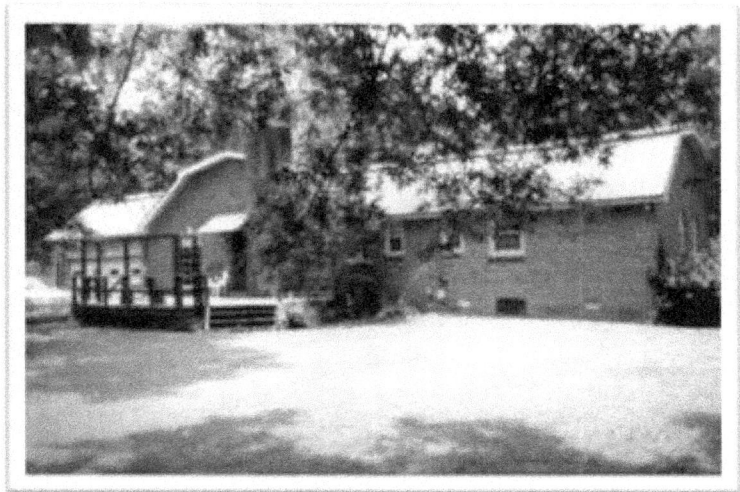

Back of House in Tullahoma

Jimmy's Nephew, Mark Shepard's Wedding

Left to Right: Shirley, Lori (Mark's Wife), Mark, Becky, Her
Husband, Vance Shepard (Mark's Parents)

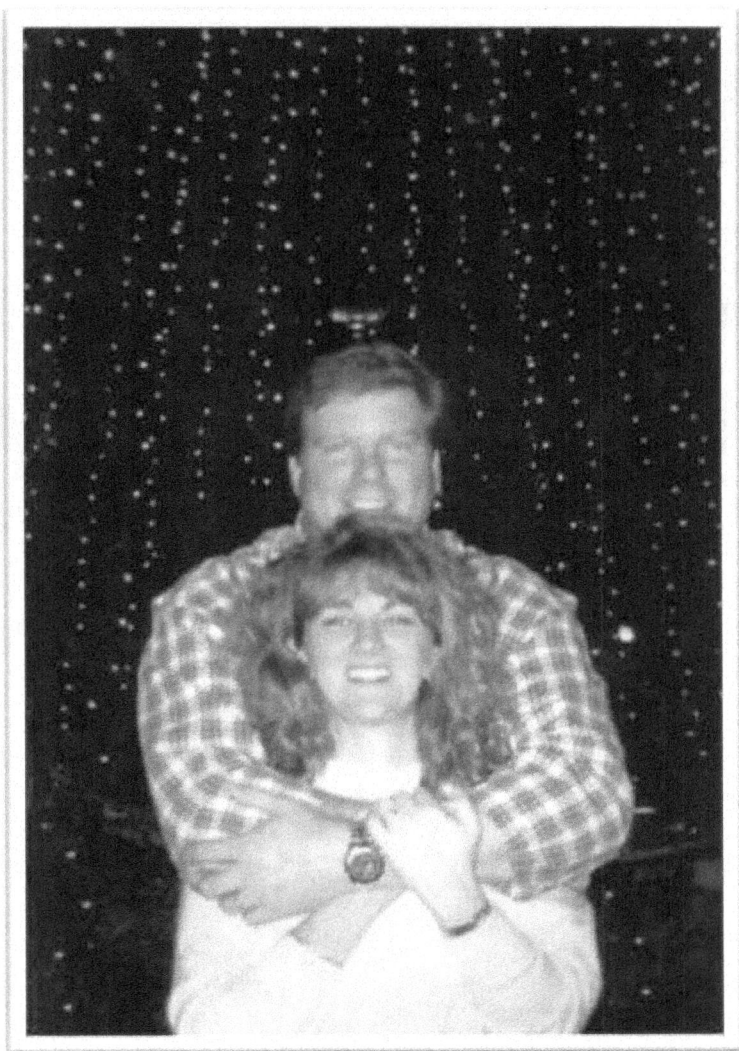

Jimmy's Nephew, Mark Shepard and Wife, Lori

Lori, Nat, Hannah and Mark Shepard, December, 2007

Nat and Hannah, Mark and Lori's "Spitzwart"
and "Mugwomp"

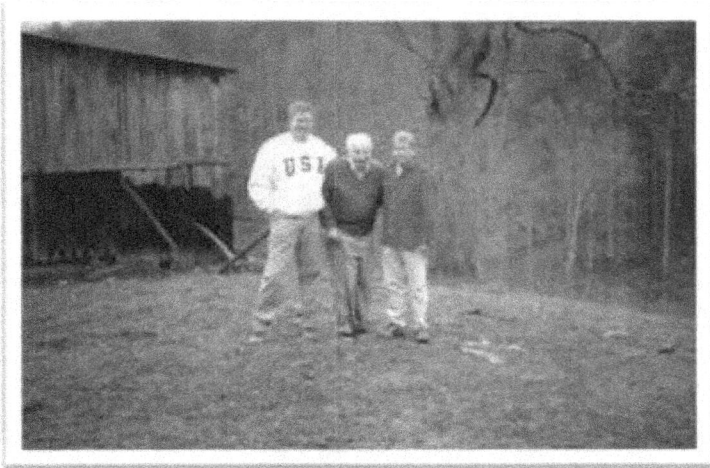

Mark Shepard , Duard Lawson and Max Shepard

Seated: Jimmy's Niece, Betty and Husband, Carroll Dennis

Standing: Tod, Andrea, Ryan and Brett

Lorene "Tysie" Lawson

"Tysie" and Duard Lawson

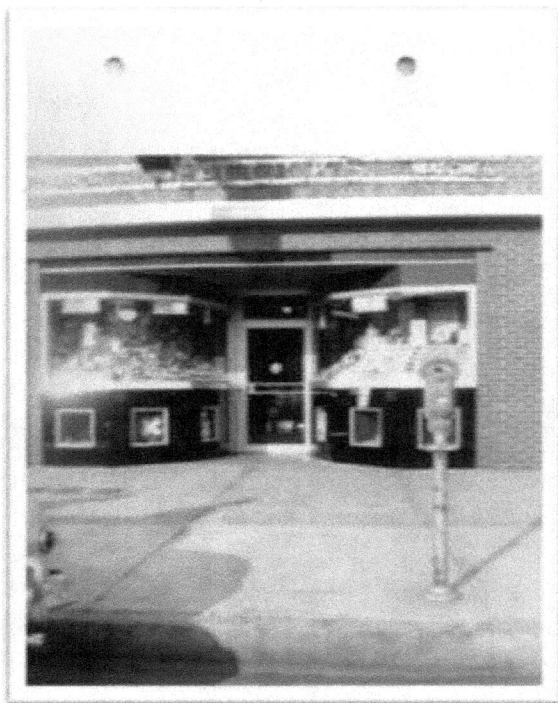

Front of Jimmy's Jewelry Store

Jimmy and Mary Louise, Serena and Claymon Stewart, Jimmy's Cousin

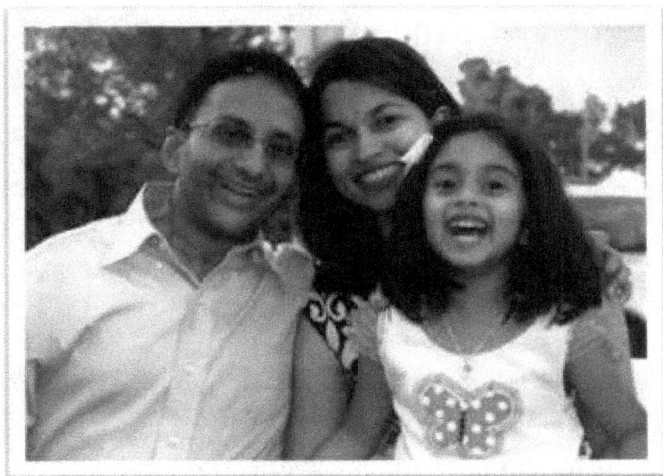

Dylan, Vanessa and Kaitlyn Lobo, 2014

Patty Lawson Blevins and Husband, Joe

Patty and Joe's Daughter, Tracy's Family, 2014

Left to Right: Luke, Mark, Tracy and Alyse Brassard

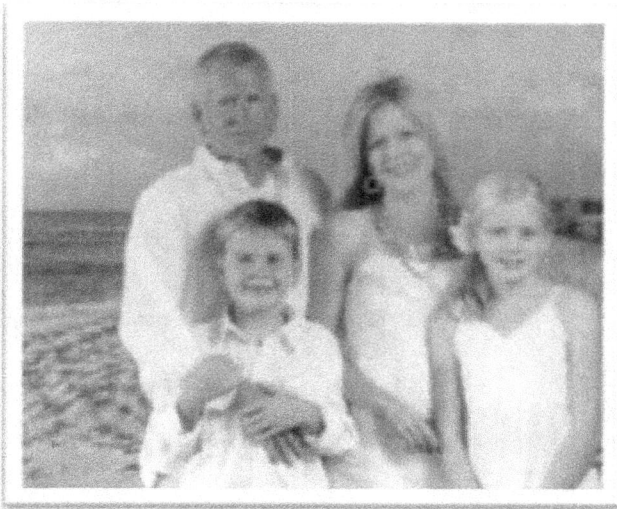

Patty and Joe's son, Max, Stacy, Austin and Maggie, 2011

Jimmy's Niece, Janet "Jan" Stewart Summer, 2007

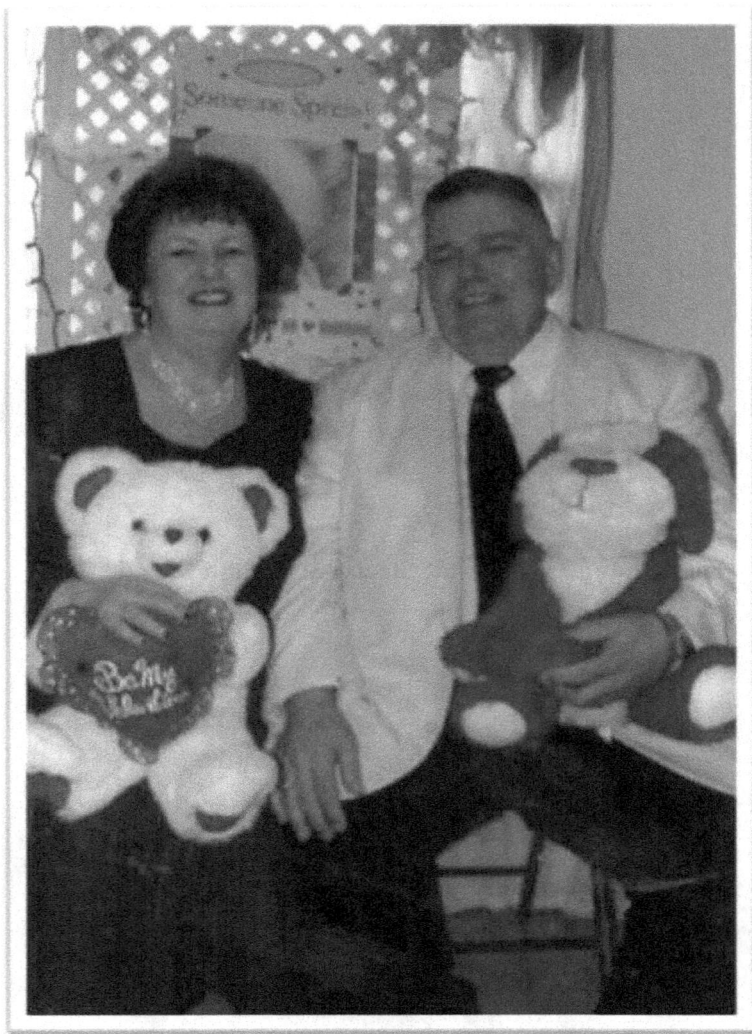

Pastor Bill and Ann Danskin, Sunlake Baptist, Florida

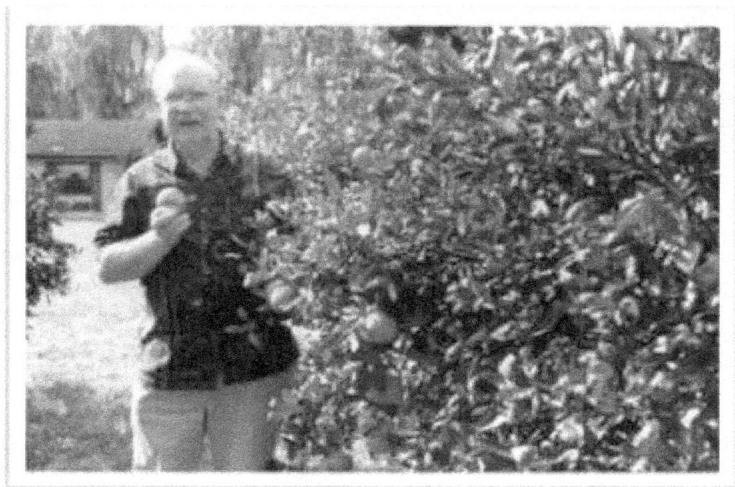

Claymon Stewart Picking Oranges at Jimmy's Florida Home, 1998

Jimmy's Home in Lutz, Florida

113

Back of Home in Lutz, Florida

Bridge Across to Island

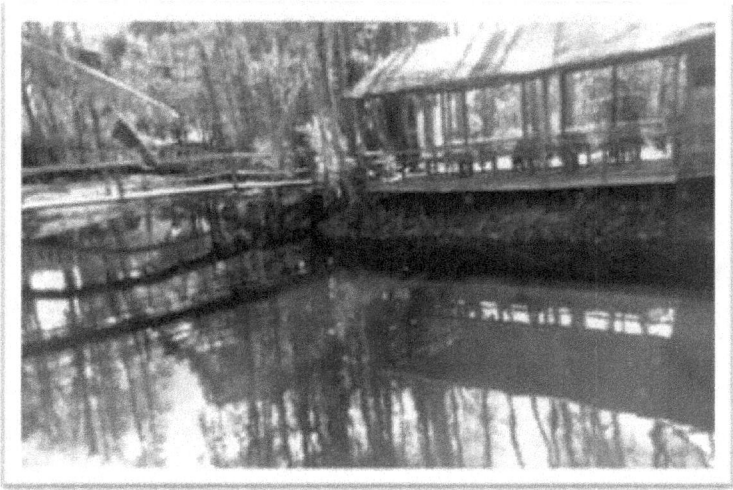

End of Bridge and Picnic Shelter

Picnic Shelter Close Up

Marbury Road Home, Tullahoma, Tennessee, Up to 2002

Jimmy with Star, Marbury Road Property

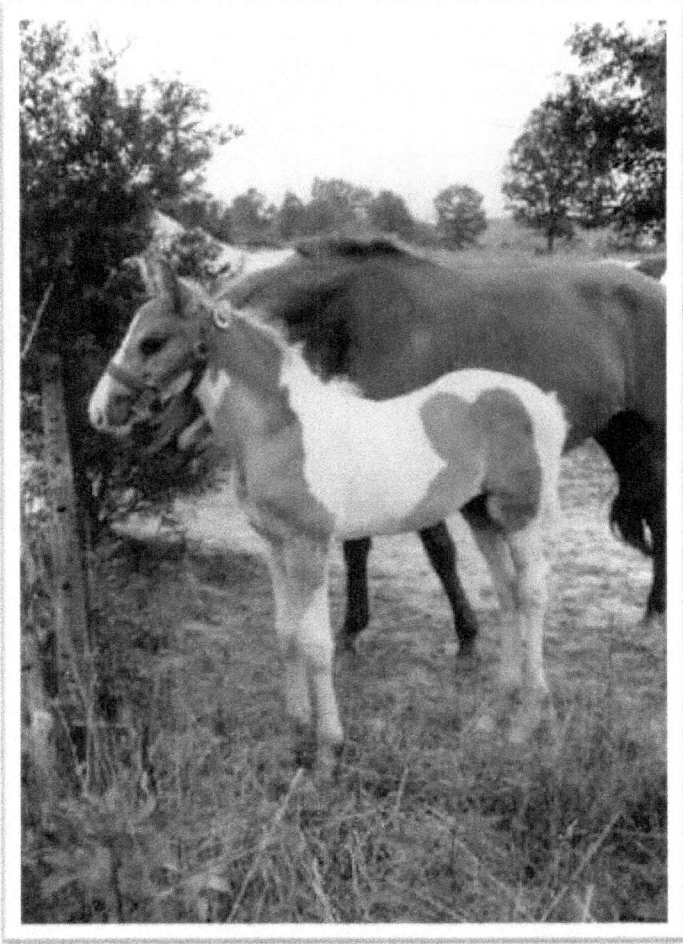

Chief and Beauty at Marbury Road

Views 1 and 2 of Florida Farm When Purchased

Mary Louise Looking at Florida Farm When Purchased

Florida Farm After Clearing, View One

Home Built by Renter on Florida Farm

Carl Tipton and Wife, Sophie

Jimmy and Mary Louise

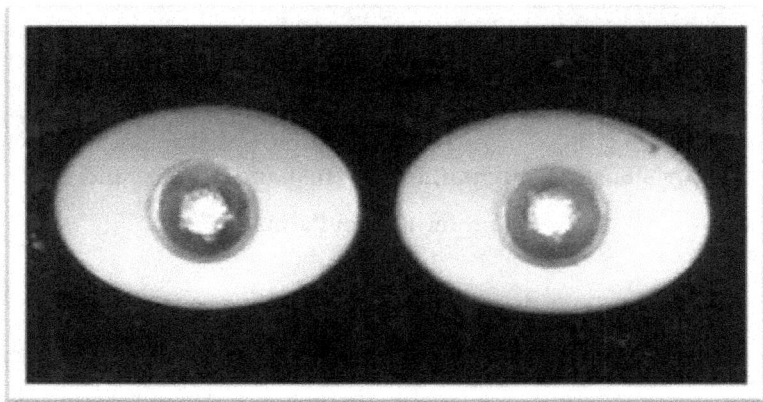

Gold Diamond Cufflinks Given to Jimmy by Mr. Lipman

Jimmy's Foster Daughter, Billie, Husband, Chuck, and Their Daughter Rachel Palmatier